This is a Dolphin

This is a Dolphin

SeaWorld Books for Young Learners

PART OF THE SEAWORLD EDUCATION SERIES

Writer
Deborah Nuzzolo

Technical Advisors
Brad Andrews
Daniel K. Odell, Ph.D.
Dudley Wigdahl

Education Directors
Lorna Crane
Hollis J. Gillespie
Bob Mindick
Sheila Voss
Joy L. Wolf

Editorial Staff
Jody Byrum
Judith Coats
Deborah Nuzzolo
Donna Parham

Photos
Bob Couey

Illustrations/Design
Doug Fulton
Salma Martin-Fardon

Dedicated to Jim Antrim, SeaWorld San Diego General Curator, upon his retirement. Your enthusiasm and dedication to sea life inspires us all. With our thanks, the Education Department.

Dolphin photos in this book

bottlenose dolphin: front cover, 4, 16, 25

Commerson's dolphin: 6, 25

common dolphin: 22, 25

false killer whale: 14, 25

killer whale: 8, 18, 25

Pacific white-sided dolphin: 12, 20, 25

pilot whale: 10, 25

ISBN 1-893698-22-X

Printed in the United States of America

©2002 Sea World, Inc. All Rights Reserved.

Published by SeaWorld San Diego
500 SeaWorld Drive, San Diego, California, 92109-7904

This is a Dolphin

SeaWorld Books for Young Learners

by Deborah Nuzzolo

This is a dolphin. It lives in the ocean.

Dolphins, in the whale family *Delphinidae*, live in all the oceans of the world. Delphinids include such well known species as the bottlenose dolphin and common dolphin as well as the killer whale.

It moves its tail in an up-and-down motion.

Each lobe of a dolphin's tail is called a fluke. The up-and-down motion of the flukes moves the dolphin forward through the water.

The blowhole on top is where it gets air.

A dolphin breathes through a single blowhole located on the top of its head. The blowhole is covered by a muscular flap, which provides a watertight seal.

Its flippers for steering come as a pair.

A dolphin's forelimbs are pectoral flippers. As it swims, a dolphin uses its pectoral flippers to steer and, with the help of the flukes, to stop.

It packs on its back a dorsal fin, too.

The dorsal fin may act as a keel. It probably helps stabilize a dolphin as it swims, but is not essential to a dolphin's balance.

Its sharp teeth catch fish, but do not chew.

A dolphin's teeth are cone-shaped and interlocking, designed for grasping, not chewing, food. A dolphin usually swallows fish whole.

A dolphin calf swims alongside its mother.

Dolphin calves are born in the water, usually tail-first. A mother dolphin stays close by and attentively directs the calf's movements.

Dolphins travel and live in groups with each other.

Dolphins are social animals; they live and travel in groups. In some types of dolphins, individuals enter and leave the group at any time. But others, like killer whales, have stable groups.

To discover what's near... they use sound.

where they are...

Dolphins produce whistles, clicks, and sounds that resemble moans, trills, grunts, and squeaks. Sound helps them navigate, communicate, and hunt.

Keep their home clean. Keep dolphins around.

Dolphins are affected by heavy boat traffic, habitat destruction, competition with fisheries, and pollution. Reduce, reuse, and recycle your trash so it doesn't end up in the ocean.

Words to Know

blowhole — the nostril(s) at the top of the head in whales, dolphins, and porpoises, through which they breathe.

calf — the young of certain large mammal species, such as whales and manatees.

communicate — to convey information.

Delphinidae — the scientific family that includes about 30 species of dolphins.

dorsal fin — the fin on the back of a whale.

flippers — the broad flat forelimbs of whales, supported by bones and adapted for swimming.

flukes — the horizontal lobes of a whale's tail, made of connective tissue (not bone).

habitat — the normal, usual, or natural place where an animal lives.

hunt — to pursue for food.

navigate — to travel by water.

ocean — the body of salt water covering nearly three-fourths of the earth's surface.

pair — *n.:* two corresponding body parts.

whale — an aquatic mammal in the scientific order Cetacea, which includes dolphins and porpoises. Whales have forelimbs modified into flippers, a horizontally flattened tail, a nostril at the top of the head for breathing, and no hindlimbs.

 bottlenose
dolphin

 Commerson's
dolphin

 common
dolphin

false killer
whale

killer whale

Pacific white-sided
dolphin

pilot whale

25

This is a Dolphin

This is a dolphin. It lives in the ocean.

It moves its tail in an up-and-down motion.

The blowhole on top is where it gets air.

Its flippers for steering come as a pair.

It packs on its back a dorsal fin, too.

Its sharp teeth catch fish, but do not chew.

A dolphin calf swims alongside its mother.

Dolphins travel and live in groups with each other.

To discover what's near... where they are... they use sound.

Keep their home clean. Keep dolphins around.

Want more information?

If you have a questions about dolphins or other animals...

◆ Call **1-800-23-SHAMU** (1-800-237-4268).
TDD users call 1-800-TD-SHAMU (1-800-837-4268).
These toll-free phone numbers are answered by the
SeaWorld Education Department.

◆ Visit the SeaWorld/Busch Gardens Animal
Information Database at *www.seaworld.org*
or *www.buschgardens.org*

◆ E-mail: shamu@seaworld.org

◆ The SeaWorld Education Department has books,
teacher's guides, posters, and videos available on a
variety of animals and topics. Call or write to request
an Education Department publications brochure,
or shop online at our e-store.

Goals of the SeaWorld and Busch Gardens Education Departments

Based on a long-term commitment to education, SeaWorld and Busch Gardens strive to provide an enthusiastic, imaginative, and intellectually stimulating atmosphere to help students and guests develop a lifelong appreciation, understanding, and stewardship for our environment. Specifically, our goals are...

- To instill in students and guests of all ages an appreciation for science and a respect for all living creatures and habitats.
- To conserve our valuable natural resources by increasing awareness of the interrelationships of humans and the environment.
- To increase students' and guests' basic competencies in science, math, and other disciplines.
- To be an educational resource to the world.

"For in the end we will conserve only what we love. We will love only what we understand. We will understand only what we are taught." — B. Dioum

SeaWorld San Diego
(800) 380-3202
500 Sea World Drive
San Diego, CA 92109-7904

SeaWorld San Antonio
(210) 523-3606
10500 Sea World Drive
San Antonio, TX 78251-3002

SeaWorld Orlando
(800) 406-2244
7007 Sea World Drive
Orlando, FL 32821-8097

Discovery Cove
(877) 434-7268
6000 Discovery Cove Way
Orlando, FL 32821-8097

Busch Gardens Tampa Bay
(813) 987-5555
P.O. Box 9157
Tampa, FL 33674-9157

Busch Gardens Williamsburg
(800) 343-7946
One Busch Gardens Blvd.
Williamsburg, VA 23187-8785